FORCED TO GROW UP

A HOLOCAUST STORY

In Honor and Memory

To the Many Family Members I Lost
During the Holocaust

FORCED TO GROW UP

A HOLOCAUST STORY

BERTA GARDON

Edited by Mihai Grunfeld

Croft Publication 2019

First Printing: 2019

ISBN: 978-0-359-38268-2

Croft Publication

http://pages.vassar.edu/mihaigrunfeldauthor/

Cover photo: *My sister Grete at age 5 and I at age 4*

Contents

MEMORIES OF VIENNA

I hear the birds singing, and before
Opening my eyes I know the sun is up.
Day is trying to enter my mind,
But I am holding on to my peaceful night.

Slowly the cadence rises,
And the dogs' barking joins the singing of the birds.
High-pitched children's voices
Add to the music of the morning.

The cars' engines sound like rolling drums,
And no longer can I pretend to be asleep.
A new day has started.
I'll take whatever comes.

July 1951

Once Upon A Time

My early childhood was spent in Vienna. From the windows of our apartment I could hear the rushing waters of the *Kleine Donau* (Little Danube), and I could see fishing boats and tourist ships on their way to far-off lands. I used to watch them until they disappeared in the distance and were nothing but a speck on the horizon. As far back as I remember, I fell asleep hearing the gurgling of the river. I spent many hours playing on the river's banks, or just sitting and watching wave after wave in endless procession. There was always something to see. As soon as the weather permitted, the grassy banks leading down to the water were filled with people basking in the sunshine. The river ran fast. Swimming was not permitted, but no one paid any attention to this prohibition. Full of glee, I watched the occasional policeman shout at the young men, in the scantiest of swim trunks, as they jumped into the water once he appeared. There was nothing he could do, so after a short time he usually departed with a red face. The boathouse located upriver disgorged young men who practiced in their shells while the coxswain's rhythmical shouts filled the air. Young couples in rowboats pretended to be fishing as they slowly floated by. To my delight, every so often a smoke-belching steamboat full of tourists chugged down the river, blasting its horn on the way to Hungary. I waved and waved and wished and dreamed to be on one of these excursion boats some day.

On sunny afternoons many pushcart vendors came by selling ice cream, nougat, pretzels piled high on a stick, watermelon, halva, and many other delights. Occasionally, a group of Gypsies arrived, their women in colorful skirts spilling out of covered wagons, doing a brisk business telling fortunes while their children begged. The old men sharpened scissors and knives and fixed pots and pans. The young men looked fierce, ready to pick a fight if any of the local young men came too near to the women. The people, and their horses, always looked dusty and tired. I felt sorry for them. The local police did not permit them to camp longer than twenty-four hours.

On hot summer nights, my family picnicked at the river's edge, waiting for the temperature to come down. The upper banks along the river were lined with trees, home to a variety of birds whose chirping woke us every morning and hushed us every evening as we listened to their song. I have pleasant memories of falling asleep to the sounds of gurgling water, laughter, and music.

Before World War II

I could hardly wait to be old enough to start school. Full of excitement and proudly carrying my new leather schoolbag, I entered first grade before my sixth birthday. My mother walked me to school at first, but after a few days I was on my own. My days were filled with stories, arts and crafts, and ten o'clock refreshments. For the obligatory nap after lunch, each child had to take a small folding lawn chair and a blanket from a huge closet. We were ordered to close our eyes, and if we could not sleep to just listen to the quietly played music. I was a very small child and remember wrestling with the lawn chair while trying to open it. At that age, mastering the opening of the chair was my only worry. Of course I knew about anti-Jewish sentiments from overhearing my parents' conversations, but did not feel it had anything to do with me. I thought this was a phase of growing up, which I would learn to handle as I got older.

Vienna is a beautiful city, greatly praised in song and romantic stories, but the memories of my early years at school are rather different. Nearly every day, as I stepped out from the security of the building we lived in, I was approached by beggars with outstretched arms. I was truly scared, but also sad because I had nothing to give them. It was my first experience with the world outside my family.

School became another shocking reality. Being called a dirty Jew, being lifted up and put on a desk with jeering children all around, filled me with fear. I had no idea what their intentions were, and I was released only when the teacher entered the classroom. Assessing the situation, my homeroom teacher, Miss Regina, cleverly arranged my protection by organizing our class into teams of two; each member of each pair was responsible for the other's well-being. It was because of her that school became a positive experience, and my devotion and admiration for her was endless. Each morning, at exactly ten o'clock, the school bell rang for our mid-morning refreshment. We received a small container of milk to enjoy with the sandwich that we were supposed to bring from home. My mother was busy with her work, making fine embroidery for an elegant store; my father's job often kept him on the road for weeks. My sister and I were frequently left on our own, and many times I forgot to bring my snack. When my teacher noticed, she always shared her sandwich with me.

At home, I had many questions. Mama, why do the other children call me a dirty Jew? "You can tell them you are Jewish but not dirty," she said. "But why do they say it then?" I asked. My mother told me that they just repeat what they hear from their parents. "But why do their parents say things like that?" My mother would reply, "Only God knows. Keep your head up and be proud of who you are." This is how I learned about the dangerous side of anti-Semitism.

My mother Manja Rost

My teammate Hanna——a strong, pretty girl with bouncy, reddish-brown curls——was always late to school. She would forget her books, and she was hopeless at math. After school, I would stop at her place, where, as our teacher had requested, I would help her with her homework. I was not very successful, but I had a great time. Hanna had all the wonderful books I wanted, she had the most contagious laughter, and was lots of fun. She was a ray of sunshine, the first friend I had outside my family, and I loved her with all my heart. After four years I was promoted to middle school but Hanna did not make it. Although we were still in the same school building, we had different teachers and classes but I always looked forward to our pleasant morning walks.

Both Hanna and I lived near a major traffic circle, I on one side and she on the other. I soon learned to dash between cars, horse-drawn wagons, and streetcars, while ignoring the conductors who tried to warn me by ringing their bells. I enjoyed picking her up each morning to help make sure she would be on time. We passed by a military establishment, several small stores with interesting window displays, large apartment buildings and restaurants, all with many exciting things to see. On our early walks, we usually arrived just as the gates of the military barracks opened. Blaring trumpets announced the exit of cavalry, as beautifully groomed horses, manes flying, snorting noisily, would greet the new day. We were careful to stay out of their path, yet we could never get enough of this thrilling and colorful sight.

Passing by the restaurants was an exciting experience. Produce and beer was delivered early in the morning. Huge Belgian horses with large heads, big hairy legs, and heavy hoofs waited patiently while kegs of beer were unloaded. The sidewalk was very narrow. I was tiny, and squeezing by the whinnying horses was extremely intimidating. Though I loved horses and was never harmed by any of them, their big heads, continuously swishing tails, large yellow teeth and wet kisses made me feel uneasy.

I loved going to school and I continued to meet Hanna every morning. One day she told me not to come to her house anymore; her parents had told her not to socialize with Jews. I was thunderstruck, thought it was a bad joke but after seeing her parents' unsmiling faces, I understood that I was not welcome anymore. It broke my heart. We had been good friends for many years, and the rejection was difficult to understand. My world began to fall apart and it took a long, long time before I was able to trust anyone again.

I was an avid reader of the daily newspaper, and the precarious situation of Jewish people in an anti-Semitic world became frighteningly clear to me. Behind the beautiful facades of Vienna there was an incredible amount of poverty. A scapegoat was needed. The various political parties fought each other, not just through newspaper articles and speeches, but also physically. Nearly every weekend, groups of drunken rowdies beat each other up. This behavior often led to knife fights, but mostly it ended with hazing and beating of Jews. The Jewish youth groups fought back. My male cousins were often in the midst of the greatest melees, and each evening, our family anxiously awaited their return.

How I admired them when listening to stories of their courageous acts! Their stories made my uncles remember their experiences of World War I, and there was much talk about survival and how different things would be if there were another war. Though we felt it was below our dignity, my cousin Kurt and I listened while we hid under a table, pretending to play house. He was my best friend and playmate, just a year and a half younger than me. I remember thinking how I would act should I ever get into any similar situations. I fully believe hearing my uncles' and cousins' stories helped me to survive the following years.

There was nothing that surprised me, and there was nothing I had not heard before.

Newspaper articles full of insults and ugly drawings showing misshapen Jews appeared daily. I started to look around, to see if any of our family or friends fitted these ugly descriptions, but I could not find any relationship to us. How dare they say that my home was not mine, the city I loved, the language I was so familiar with and was able to use like a musical instrument? Where did this hate come from? For a twelve-year-old girl this was difficult to understand. From the windows of our apartment I could see the Danube, its banks filled with people having a good time. I loved to watch the smoke-belching paddlewheel boats, filled with happy people coming down the river on their way to Budapest, and I wished I could be one of the vacationers. In the distance, I could see a row of mountains, knowing that there were the Vienna woods so greatly praised in music and songs. Many evenings I watched the sun set behind these mountains, outlining them with a band of gold. It was the place I loved, the place I was born in and whose beauty I still remember.

The German propaganda machine became more and more vicious. It became clear that it was only a matter of time before Austria would be engulfed in war. Without much hope, Jewish youth groups assisted in the resistance to the German takeover. Machine guns were mounted on rooftops, and shots were exchanged across the Danube Canal and other parts of the city. The greatest resistance existed in the residential areas, and my mother feared stray shots coming through the windows. I remember all of us lying on the floor of our apartment.

The situation deteriorated daily. The general population became strongly influenced by the hateful propaganda. People we had known for years started to make cutting, unkind remarks against Jews. Our neighbor, who had always professed her love for me, suddenly spouted political slogans and made me feel very uneasy. Her apartment was decorated with swastikas; she even hung them from her Christmas tree. Her behavior hurt, disturbed, and shocked me. Though I was a rather shy child, I remember finding the courage to question the meaning of swastikas and the reason for this rise of hate against Jews. "This has nothing to do with you," our neighbor said. "It's the other Jews who are bad for this country." I was perplexed, but came to the conclusion that if she accused other Jews of wrongdoing it would not be long before she would turn against me as well. I started to keep my distance and was very sad.

Religious education was obligatory in the Austrian school system, and each week a priest and a rabbi came to instruct us. Jews and Catholics went to different rooms; the few Protestants in my class were ignored. At the end of our religious sessions the two groups reunited in our homeroom. I thought that studying religion would fill our hearts with kindness but the result was just the opposite. Our rabbi instructed us in the Hebrew alphabet, told biblical stories, and tested our ability in reading Hebrew texts. I have no idea what the priest told his students but when the two groups were reunited we looked with curious apprehension at each other while animosity filled the air.

School continued as usual, except for air raid tests. We had drills nearly every day. When sirens sounded, students had to dive under their desks while teachers covered the windows with wet sheets against the possibility of gas attacks. I always wondered if this would work, but did not mention my fears. There was talk of war between Germany and Austria, but it was just talk.

In May of 1938, when I was thirteen years old, German military forces entered the country. They met with no resistance, and marched straight through to Vienna. The radio shouted slogans, marching music, and promises of a better life for every Austrian citizen as soon as they were rid of the Jewish scum. I was worried, afraid, and much shaken but still hoped that all this terrible propaganda was only politics as usual. Our mother said we should not go downtown, but my sister and I wanted to see the soldiers marching in. We needed to personally understand what was happening. There we were, two little girls, seeing rows and rows of heavily armed men with boots stomping in unison; their bayonets attached, singing the "Horst Wessel Song," singing of seeing "Jewish blood spray from the tips of their knives." Very frightened, we rushed home, realizing that the life we knew was over. At the end of the school year we settled in for an uneasy summer. We were not surprised to receive a note that Jewish students were not to return to classes anymore.

My Teenage Years

It was no longer safe to leave the house. There were beatings and arrests; people disappeared. Many of our friends and family were forced to scrub the sidewalks on their knees, surrounded by cheering onlookers. Anyone could be grabbed and kicked; anyone could disappear. Neighbors could not be trusted.

Many people in the Jewish community, including my parents, thought that only men would be endangered, that women would not be harmed. Some of the men in our family left Vienna. My father, some older male cousins, and one uncle set off without any plans except the idea that we were to follow at a later time. They left the younger children and women behind.

Young hoodlums started to search Jewish apartments to see what they could find. Knowing that my mother was politically active, I was very frightened when I found a hidden bundle of anti-Nazi pamphlets. This could have been a death sentence for all three of us. She promised to get rid of them, but I was never certain that she did. We soon ran out of money. Luckily, my mother had many skills and was able to support us by making her beautiful embroidery. She sat there day and night stitching, though this barely made ends meet. Each evening, we counted the money she had made, knowing very well that we needed to save some for the day we had to leave. Very soon it became clear that we could not stay; it was just too dangerous to be seen and recognized.

The men had their own excitement. They were arrested on their way out of Austria for not having an exit permit or visa to any other country. My father had the foresight to have taken along the various medals he had received as a veteran of World War I. He was a gregarious, jolly man and managed to talk himself out of a dangerous situation. The old soldier in charge was also a veteran and, though he showed no sympathy for my cousins and my uncle George, put my father on a train to Italy. This, of course, was wonderful for my father. He spent some time in Italy and eventually found a smuggler to get him into Switzerland, where he remained throughout the war. To my mother's deepest regret we were unable to join him at that time.

My father Benjamin Rost as young man during World War I

Two of my cousins, brothers Siggy and Hermann escaped, somehow managed to get to Belgium, and settled in Brussels. My uncle and my cousin Benno simply disappeared after their arrest. We had no idea what had happened to them until many months later, when we received word from a concentration camp in the south of France. After a short time we were informed of my uncle's death. Benno managed to escape from the camp and came back to Vienna with awful stories of death and deprivation, only hinting at the way my uncle died. His stories gave me nightmares for many years. He stayed with us until he felt mentally and physically recuperated. After he regained his strength, he and the extended family became involved in making new plans for his escape. Just before the *Anschluss* (annexation), Benno was inducted into the Austrian army and given his uniform. The country was bristling with uniformed German and Austrian soldiers, and we all thought that one more soldier would not make any difference. Benno agreed. He dressed in his uniform, took his skis, and traveled to the Austrian border pretending to be on border patrol. It was a few tense days before we heard that he had safely arrived in Switzerland. From there he continued to Belgium, where he connected with family, and then to Antwerp, where he reconnected with his girlfriend who later became his wife. Belgium seemed to be a safe haven.

Life in Vienna became very difficult and dangerous. Our cousins in Belgium urged us to follow them. They had found people willing to help. Once all the arrangements were made it was up to us.

It was not an easy decision to leave our home, but there was no other solution. Many Jewish people were trying to sell their belongings, and my mother received very little for our apartment, the furniture, and the rest of our personal possessions. One night my mother, my sister, and I each packed a rucksack with some necessities and, with heavy hearts, we left our home, never to return. We did not know if we would ever see our extended family again.

My mother Manja Rost, my sister Grete, and I

We boarded a train that took us from Vienna across Germany to the vicinity of the Dutch border, but not so near that we would arouse suspicion. The train was full of German soldiers in heavy gear, loudly celebrating the easy annexation of Austria. Their talk was sprinkled with anti-Semitic remarks. We were frightened, but we managed not to arouse suspicion. Pretending to be Austrian tourists wanting to see the new Fatherland, we talked about the pleasures of our trip, the sights, and we tried to be as casual as possible. I remember the relief I felt when we arrived at our pre-planned destination and got off the train. We just stood there for a while, not knowing how to proceed. We had some extremely anxious moments until, finally, a man greeted us by mentioning our cousins' name and took us to a place where we could spend the night. It was difficult to put our life and security into a stranger's hands. The hours passed slowly, and we were unable to sleep, listening to each little noise.

Leaving

The next morning, at a specified time, we were to walk to the border between Germany and Holland and demand to cross by mentioning our cousins' name. With heavy hearts, we did as instructed. My mother divided the rest of the money we still had between the three of us. When we were separated, I was terrified and immediately gave my money to an armed soldier who growled, "Give me your money." My mother was taken to a nearby building. My sister had a bad head cold. She was constantly blowing her nose into a large very dirty handkerchief, and no one went near her. It seemed to be hours before my mother reappeared. My heart beat with relief. They let us go, and we entered Holland. There we stood with only three rucksacks and a handful of money wrapped in my sister's dirty handkerchief. My mother never told us what had happened, and we did not ask.

What were we to do now? We walked away from the German border; afraid someone would come after us. My fear mounted when

I noticed a black car trailing us. We were ready to run. But when the driver stopped and the door opened, there was our cousin Siggy. He had left the security of Belgium to meet us and see that we were safe. Our relief was immense, but we were not yet out of the woods. The German border was too near and at times soldiers came across investigating the neighborhood. We were not safe yet. We still had to get across Holland to the border with Belgium and then to Brussels.

Arrangements had been made for us to spend the night at a nearby farm. We enjoyed being able to wash and sleep in clean beds. The next morning we ate a sumptuous breakfast. We were given delicious food, much of it items that we had not seen for some time. I could not believe it—there was even chocolate for my sister and me. We looked for our cousin but were informed that he had settled the bill and returned to Belgium after arranging the next stage of our escape. We had to leave that same afternoon. I wanted to stay a few more days, just a few more days of feeling secure in a warm home. I begged my mother to arrange it, but this was not an option; it would endanger all of us as well as our hosts. We were driven some distance, past fields and fields of tulips flowering in all the colors of the rainbow. Then we had to get out of the car to walk toward the border between Holland and Belgium. The driver, not wanting to expose himself to any danger, promised to meet us again on the other side and take us to Brussels. It was an ominous sign, and I was afraid that we would once again be separated from my mother. But this time the crossing went without difficulty.

This photo was taken when I lived in Belgium, when wearing the start became law. Even though the law also existed in France, in an effort to escape there, I no longer wore the star

Belgium

Once we were in Belgium, the driver picked us up and, as promised, drove straight to Brussels. We arrived hungry and tired, without money and fearful of the future. But I dreamt of coming back one day to see those wonderful fields of flowering tulips again. My sister, Grete, age fourteen, was the only one of us able to speak a few words of school-girl French. In the beginning, that was our only connection to life around us. I had opted to take English in school, but all I had learned up to then were the most basic phrases. These were of no use in Belgium. Some of our relatives had arrived before us, and had rented a narrow three-story house. We were welcomed with open arms and tears of joy. It became immediately clear to us that our stay could only be temporary. The house was fully occupied, with two families on the first floor, two families on the second floor, and Siggy's mother, my aunt Fannie on the third floor. Aunt Fannie's room was also the kitchen, and during the day the whole family seemed to congregate there. Altogether there were sixteen of us, including two friends who had no other place to go, housed in a five-room house that had only one bathroom. No one had any

privacy. After a few weeks, my mother decided it was time to move.

Oldest Aunt, Tante Fannie, who lived in the top floor of the house with five bedrooms in Brussels. All living in the house congregated with her in the small room which also served as the family kitchen

Cousin Siggy found us a furnished room that had a kitchenette. It

was not expensive, but still more than we could afford. He paid for the first two weeks, while my mother tried to orient herself. She befriended a restaurant owner who was willing to hire her on a trial basis. It was a sleepy place, catering mostly to a drinking clientele. My mother realized that most immigrants had no place to keep house, and she promised the owner more customers looking for a place to eat and meet. Very soon, through her efforts, the small restaurant became a meeting place for many of our old and new friends, and my mother had a new profession as a cook. My beautiful teenage cousin Melanie also worked there, selling her homemade candy, six to eight sugar frosted grapes on a stick that exploded in incredible sweetness in one's mouth.

Life took on a semblance of normalcy. Very soon, some more of my young cousins and friends arrived in Brussels, and I did not feel so lonely anymore. We spent a lot of time walking around the city, getting to know the neighborhood, admiring the beautifully decorated store windows, rich department stores unlike anything we had ever seen before. We rode the elevators up and down, wondering at the different customs we observed. I spoke neither French nor Flemish (the two languages of Belgium) and was surrounded by voices without understanding anything I heard. I felt like the only fish in a sea of sound, separated from the rest of the world. It was an eerie experience.

A whole summer passed this way, and in the autumn of 1939 the family decided that my cousin Kurt and I should register for school. By then Kurt was nearly thirteen years old, and I was fourteen. At that time, obligatory education in Belgium ended at age sixteen, and Kurt's sister

Berta (in our family we had three Bertas) and my sister Grete were considered too old.

School was a traumatic experience. Our command of French was minimal, so we could not communicate. No one bothered to teach us the language. The only classes we participated in were mathematics and music, where no language was needed. The nuns were friendly but indifferent; the students ignored us. Our parents had hoped that we would find friends to protect us, but we spoke the language of the hated German enemy and found no acceptance. We did not belong, nor did we want to be separated from our families for the whole day. With so many people constantly disappearing, we worried all the time if our parents would still be there when we returned from school. We begged our parents to let us stay home, and they agreed that our education had to be put on hold.

The political situation did not improve. The German army attacked and occupied Czechoslovakia and Poland. More and more Jewish immigrants came through Belgium on their way to safety. They all needed a place to stay, and they all had terrible stories of persecution. My mother had a big heart. Our small place, barely big enough for us, had people sleeping on chairs, on the table and on the floor. It seemed that everyone knew about our place and, as soon as one family left, some other strangers showed up. To our joy, one day our grandfather arrived at our door, along with some more cousins and my fathers' youngest sister, my aunt Jenny. Money was scarce; we lived from day to day. There was no way my mother could provide kosher food for my grandfather, and he decided to continue to Antwerp, where he found a large community of Orthodox Jews.

My Grandfather

I was not quite six years old when I met my grandfather for the first time. All nine of my mother's siblings had stories to tell. According to them, he was tall and strong, and always fair and kind—but most of all he was extremely devout. After his first wife's death he had married again and moved to his new wife's hometown. One day, the family council was called together—disaster had struck. My grandfather's second wife had died. He informed his nine children that he was coming to live with them, on a rotating basis. He would spend a few months here, a few months there.

My grandfather Menachim Schleier who disappeared during the Holocaust

Every home in the family was scrubbed, cleaned, and koshered in the hope of finding my grandfather's approval. At the same time, each one of my aunts and uncles searched far and wide to find a new wife for their father. I looked forward to finally meeting my grandfather, but also feared his arrival. I was just five years old, and I could not understand how one man could so disturb the mental equilibrium of all the adults in my family. What was the power he had over them?

The great day arrived. With all the excitement, no one had noticed my feverish eyes, coughing and sore throat. Finally my fever rose so high I became delirious and was put to bed. First came the doctor and then, you guessed it, my grandfather. This was the first time I had met him, and in my feverish state, I could not believe that this was the man everyone feared. He was smiling as he bent over me with his long, long white beard. I was convinced that God had come to visit. He was also very strong. With a flip of his fingers he ripped the cord that held his suitcase together. I had never seen anyone so strong. My mother desperately tried to convince me that it was only Grandfather, but it was to no avail. My temperature rose and fell, and I went in and out of consciousness. At one moment I was seeing my grandfather, the next moment seeing God as he was described in my picture books. Then this apparition pulled a handful of sticky candy out of his coat pocket and said, "*Nem, nem!* Take, take!"

I recuperated quickly enough, but could not shake the idea that I had seen God until I was formally introduced to my grandfather, and he, smilingly, pulled a handful of sticky candy out of his pocket and said, "*Nem, nem!* Take, take!"

My aunts found an elderly lady willing to be my grandfather's third wife, and they were married after a few weeks. His only request was that she kept a kosher home. Even to me it was obvious that this was not a love match, and I was puzzled why people of such advanced age were getting married. Theirs was a serene relationship, and it taught me the importance of companionship.

Grandfather came to visit us often, yet never reprimanded my mother for not keeping a kosher kitchen. I always watched with amazement as he emptied his pockets, a can of sardines from one, and a hard-boiled egg from another. All he asked for was a glass plate. Then we watched him eat. With each mouthful he would say, "Ah, what a *machaie* (pleasure)!"

My grandfather was a lay leader of a small synagogue, a true believer. None of his children had followed in his path. Though we celebrated all the Jewish holidays according to tradition, our lifestyle was not to his expectation. I knew he was very disappointed, yet he showed nothing but love to his grandchildren. I very much wanted to please him and, though my mother thought at age seven I was too young, I decided to fast for Yom Kippur, the Jewish Day of Atonement. Grandfather, the judge of all that happened in our family, looked at me and declared, "You are too young, too skinny, and you are just a girl. Girls don't have to fast!" Just to show him that I was as good as any boy, I fasted. He smiled! The last time I saw him was when he was on his way to Antwerp.

My Aunt Jenny had recently been married and was expecting a child. Her husband had been arrested by the Germans and had disappeared without a trace. None of us had proper documents; we could not get permission to work and, though we had to register, we were considered illegal residents. It was so ironic that in Austria, the country of our birth, we were undesirable aliens, Jews. And in Belgium, we were undesirable and unwanted Germans. We were sitting between a rock and a hard place.

Difficult Decisions

In 1940, the German army attacked France, Holland, and Belgium. The Maginot Line, a line of fortified bunkers between Germany and France that was supposed to protect France, held only for a very short while before being overrun by German forces. There was some resistance in Holland, but we knew it was only a matter of days before the enemy would be in Belgium. More people fleeing ahead of the German army arrived at our door. I remember one young couple and their lovely little girl with long, dark braids and big dark eyes. How I hoped she would have a chance to grow up. Because of the daily stress, the scarcity of food, and the uncertainty of the future, I became preoccupied with thoughts of death. At that time, I decided that, should I be so lucky as to survive, I was going to have children. Our family members were hiding in various places; my mother, my sister, and I thought we had a chance to escape. We had heard that the withdrawing English soldiers were being picked up by a flotilla of small boats all along the French coastline, and we hoped to find a spot on one of these boats to England. With several of my aunts and cousins, we started on our walk to catch up with the retreating army. The roads were full of people, cars, baby buggies, horse-drawn carts, all filled with belongings of people wanting to escape.

We heard shooting in the distance and there was an uneasy mood in the crowd. Suddenly we heard the drone of airplanes. We looked up and saw several Stukas, the infamous German fighter planes, sweeping down towards the road. We were under attack. My mother yelled, "Into the woods!" and we took off towards the safety of the trees, crouching in their dark shade, listening to the rat-tat of machine guns, fearful to be seen. Then it fell quiet, until we heard wailing and cries. People began to pick up their belongings, leaving the injured and dead behind.

The march continued, and after this experience we cautiously walked along the edge of the road, so as to have less of a sprint to the safety of the trees. Once, while we were walking, my mother suddenly said, "Don't look up, you don't want to see that!" Of course I looked up, but I saw nothing; only much later did I realize that she did not want me to see the carnage on the road. Some of my aunts could not walk as fast as the younger people and, after arranging a meeting place, we separated. It was a sad good-bye. I did not think we would see each other again.

We continued this way across France for several days, in and out of small villages until we reached the sea. There were no boats to be seen. The last boat had just left. We were disappointed, but we meant to try again the next day. We had caught up with the retreating English army, but the Germans were not far behind. The sound of gunfire was continuous and frightening.

We passed some English outposts, which were manned with just a few soldiers who were supposed to delay the enemy and give more of their comrades a chance to escape. The sun shone bright but my heart was heavy. These nice, friendly young men knew what lay ahead of them, and so did we. We would not see each other again: Will they survive? Will we? After sharing their food rations with us, they pointed to a deserted, partly destroyed house where we could stay the night. We were so very tired. By then our family group had shrunk to eight members: three adults and five children. The children were my cousins Kurt and Berta, my sister Grete, the baby Willie, and me. The rest of the family was behind German lines. Throughout the night we heard shooting, the explosions of bombs and the unnerving screams of Stuka planes on the attack. My mother, Aunt Helen and cousin Franzie (Willie's mother) thought it would be safer in the basement but after looking at it, my sister and I decided to take our chances on the upper floor. The dark, damp, partly ruined basement gave us the feeling of a grave just waiting for its occupants. I did not know it then, but the flotilla of small boats we had tried to reach in May 1940 was part of the Battle of Dunkirk and the evacuation of Allied soldiers on French soil. Thousands of soldiers were saved and brought home to fight again some other day.

Uncle Paul, his wife Aunt Helen—my mother's sister—and their daughter Berta

who disappeared during the Holocaust

Finally the night was over, and with morning came an eerie quiet. Then we heard a roar of engines and loud voices shouting instructions. Though it was not a surprise, we were shocked to see German soldiers, bristling with weapons, riding on motorcycles into town. Just then, my sister insisted that her dress was wrinkled and she absolutely had to iron it. She ran all over the house like a demented woman, looking for an iron. We tried to reason with her but then, recognizing the ridiculous irony of her behavior, we all started laughing. We laughed hysterically, with tears running down our cheeks, and eventually she joined in. All our nerves were on edge.

The military lost no time in occupying the small town. A flag emblazoned with the dreaded and reviled swastika was raised on the tallest building. We all waited for further developments. We had no food, nor any money. My sister, my cousin Berta, and I went out to see what we could find. We figured that three young, nice-looking girls would not arouse any suspicion. The soldiers were not much older than we were, and it was not difficult to befriend them. Of course we did not tell them that we were Jewish, nor did we mention that we were trying to escape. In fact, we did not let on that we understood German and could follow their conversation. It was a tense situation: the soldiers expected goodwill from the population in exchange for food.

We went down to the seashore; it was empty, and we found out that the last boat had sunk. How lucky for us that we did not manage to get on it! We searched for the place where we had seen the outpost of

English soldiers, but there was nothing to be found. It was all so sad and desolate; there was nothing but destruction all around us. We were strangers, with no connections to this place, so there was no sense in staying any longer. There was no hope that we could escape across the English Channel. The best we could do was to return to Brussels, where we hoped to find some of our relatives and friends. We were tired, bone weary, and discouraged. We dreaded the long trek back. Overhearing some of the soldiers' conversations, we found out that there was a military convoy going to the Belgian border. Without much hope of success, we asked one of the drivers if it would be possible for some of us to ride with them. To our surprise two drivers agreed, as long as we were willing to sit on their load of bombs. It was a hair-raising, rough, and jarring ride. Having been told that the bombs were not armed did nothing to reduce our stress and fear. A direct hit would have blown us sky high. Though we were relieved that we did not have to walk all the way, we were even happier to arrive at the Belgian border and get off the lorry.

From the border, we took public transportation, a network of connecting trams, back to Brussels. Over time, one by one, some of our friends and family found their way back. None of us had managed to leave the European mainland. It was clear we were going to be there for the duration of the war.

My sister had grown into a beautiful young woman. Most of the young men hanging around our place flirted with her. One of them asked my mother for permission to court her. She was just seventeen years old; he was twenty-eight. In spite of the large difference in age, my mother consented. We were in the middle of a war; it was impossible to foresee the future. Max Ruthen, called Macki, was a wonderful man. He was kind, patient, and full of humor—and good-looking, too. He loved my sister, he was kind to our mother, and he teased me endlessly. We all loved him—I was totally smitten.

Marriage certificate of my sister Grete with husband Max (1942). Max did not survive

Grete did not resist his charms very long, and after a few months became Mrs. Ruthen. There was very little we could give her, but each family member and all our friends chipped in as best they could. My mother and my aunts cooked and baked cookies, and Macki's friends donated a case of wine. The wedding was a happy affair, with my sister giggling and slightly drunk on champagne. It was the last happy family event for a very long time.

The German occupation became tougher. New regulations were announced daily: an 8:00 p.m. curfew, then food rationing, then food stamps. The wearing of a yellow star became law, and there were no food stamps for Jews. My mother insisted our yellow star should be nicely finished to show our pride. Proud we were, but also afraid. My brother-in-law went out each morning, wheeling and dealing on the black market in an effort to provide the necessities. It was extremely dangerous, but the only way to obtain food. We wore the yellow star, our papers were stamped *Juif*, Jew. We obeyed the curfew and, though we had very little to eat, we found comfort in each other. Once in a while we received much-needed food packages that my father managed to send through the Red Cross from Switzerland. I especially remember receiving sugar, a precious commodity that we could exchange for other necessities.

I was not yet fifteen years old when I joined the Zionist movement. It was a wonderful time for me, with serious talk on survival but also with singing, dancing, and learning. Suddenly, I had many good friends. Our group made many forays into the woods; we shared what little food we had, played survival games, and learned to not be afraid. I felt strong and capable.

One especially dear friend I met through the Zionist connection was named Edith. She was one year older than I, and worked illegally in a small leather factory, producing handbags, wallets, and belts. She introduced me to her boss; I feigned familiarity with an electric leather sewing machine and was hired. I had no idea what I was supposed to do, but it was necessary for me to do my share to support the family. I had never used a sewing machine and had no idea in what way a leather machine was different. I sat down and promptly ran the fat, triangular needle through my finger. I didn't make a sound, for fear of losing the job. I reversed the wheel to get the needle out. But I learned fast.

Because of the early curfew, I sometimes could not get home, so I spent many nights with Edith and her mother. They were from Berlin, not Jewish, had regular papers, and did not need to wear the yellow star. However, her father being Jewish wore the star, and was arrested while out walking with his family because it was forbidden for Jews to consort with Aryans. He was sent to a concentration camp in the south of France. They had as difficult a time as the rest of us, except that they had befriended two German soldiers and, through them, received occasional food packages and mail from their family in Berlin. The soldiers were young and lonely, and they enjoyed that we spoke their language. They visited often, and I was always afraid they would find out I was Jewish. This topic was never mentioned, though Edith talked much about her father and shared her joy when one of his rare letters arrived. It seemed the young men did not want to know what was happening—and I was grateful for the occasional sausage and loaf of bread. When I went home, my mother usually asked if I had eaten and, though I was always hungry I always said yes. Only then, would she eat the slice of bread she had kept for me. It was never much; I wished I had more to give her. Seeing my mother so hungry increased my own pain.

Hunger hurts! First, the stomach makes uncontrollable and embarrassingly loud noises, and then muscles start to cramp. After a few days a not-unpleasant heat radiates from the center of the body. Then come the headaches, then the eyes begin to hurt, and after some time one gets so light-headed that everything becomes a blur. Hallucinating, it seems one can see and understand life much clearer than ever before. Once, while passing in front of a restaurant where my cousin Mella worked, seeing and smelling all this uneaten food, I fainted. I have no idea how she brought me indoors, but I woke up to a steaming cup of coffee and a piece of bread. Mella had surely saved my life; being picked up by the police would have meant never to be seen again. Fate must have guided my steps. I had no idea that my cousin was working in the restaurant.

Another time I missed the curfew while still far from home. It was a dark night. My options were either to take off the yellow star and get on the trolley, or to keep it on, pretending to be a political dissenter. Taking off the yellow star and being found without proper papers was too dangerous; it meant immediate arrest and being shipped off to a concentration camp. I remembered having read of young people in Holland protesting the German occupation by wearing the yellow star. This made the occupying regime sufficiently concerned that they were warning soldiers of possible guerrilla actions. I hoped that, should I run into armed soldiers, they would think that the demonstrations had spread to Belgium, and that I was a dissenter, with more people hidden in the dark streets around me. Suddenly, I heard nailed boots hitting the pavement. There was no place to hide; running was out of the question—fleeing would invite being shot. The stomp of boots came nearer; bringing into sight a single armed soldier on patrol. I also wore nailed boots and defiantly stomped as loud as I could. We never left our path; as he approached I focused on his eyes, held them without blinking. Should he have decided to shoot, I wanted him to live with the knowledge of having murdered a very young civilian. We passed each other and it took all my willpower not to turn around to see if he raised his rifle. I felt totally exposed, cold sweat running down my back. When the stomping receded it became suddenly quiet. Only then did I start to run, my heart pounding as if it wanted to jump out of my chest. I reached home unable to talk about my experience. I think both of us the young soldier and I, were equally shocked and afraid. He did not look much older than I.

It did not look like the war would be ending soon; it was clear that many of us would not make it. We were permanently hungry. At night, English bombers and fighter planes droned over Brussels on their way to Germany, and the sky lit up with antiaircraft fire. The noise rattled our nerves while fear loosened our guts. My sister and I were losing our hair, probably as a result of malnutrition and stress. Though we feared the danger of nightly raids, we nevertheless welcomed them. They were our only hope of an eventual end to the madness around us.

People were disappearing at an alarming rate.

Aunt Jenny, my father's youngest sister, was pregnant and lived in a basement not far from us. I spent many nights with her so she would not be alone, and worried what I should do in case the baby arrived. I was fifteen-and-a-half years old and not much help. With blackout enforced, we both feared the hordes of mice whose basement we had taken over. We feared them showing up as soon as it got dark and we talked throughout many nights, prodding up our courage. I remember her with hair wrapped in a turban, broom in hand, banging on the floor when the mice became too noisy. Neither of us could sleep. Aunt Jenny didn't come home one evening, and I never saw her again.

My friend Edith became engaged to an eighteen-year-old Jewish boy. I told her that I thought it was the wrong time for love; we needed to concentrate on survival. Her mother thought they were too young, but gave her permission, not "wanting to deprive the young people from the only happiness they may ever have." Shortly afterward, the young man was arrested and sent to a concentration camp. Edith thought he would be helpless and followed him. They were lovely, loyal people; I never found out what happened to them.

One day I found my place of work boarded up: my boss had disappeared. I found different work, this time in a cigarette factory. The tobacco came from butts collected by children from the city's pavements. As smokers tossed their cigarettes away, the children picked them up and sold them to the highest bidder. I opened the butts, mixed the tobacco and stuffed it into new paper shells, then put them into boxes and got them ready for the market. It was a disgusting experience that made me never want to smoke, and I never did.

We needed more money to survive. For a short time, all of us—my sister, my cousin Berta, and I—worked at the same place. The owner bought old knitted items of all sorts on the black market, old socks and sweaters, any kind of material that could be unraveled. My job was to tie bits and pieces of thread together, then spun it on an old-fashioned, foot-propelled spinning wheel until there was a full bobbin. Then start again on a new skein, and on and on, all day long, the thread cutting deep into my thumb. The bobbins were sold to factories, to be dyed and reused. The pay was minimal, but the Belgian boss knew we were Jewish and treated us with kindness—and we were safe while in his employ.

The Jewish community grew smaller and smaller. Many of our friends and acquaintances disappeared after being arrested during raids. Some of them managed to let us know what had happened to them and where they were taken. We had no illusions; we knew the danger we faced. One day, I had the misfortune to get caught in a raid. I was lucky; I was let go but had to show my papers. Several days later, I received a telegram from the Gestapo to present myself immediately at the railroad station, with a blanket and basic necessities. We all knew what this meant; it was a death sentence. I had no intention of answering the summons. I was sixteen years old, and not ready to die.

Macki, my brother-in-law, knew his way around the black market. He knew where one could buy an old French passport and how to fabricate a new existence. I removed the person's picture, stuck on my own, worked on repairing the stamp so it could pass inspection, and smudged it with ashes to blur the changes. The other entry that needed to be changed was my place of birth. Somehow it had to be explained why a French citizen spoke with a German accent and was not fully fluent in French. I became a resident of the Alsace, a region in northeastern France that had, over the centuries, been disputed, with annexation back and forth between France and Germany. Many of the residents of Alsace spoke only German.

Now that I had a passport, we needed to find a guide to help me on the way to get out of Belgium, maybe to Spain or Switzerland. My brother-in-law paid a large sum of money to a woman who promised to take me to a safe place. The deal was made, and it was time to part from my family. My mother wept, as did all the rest of us. My sister took an anchor pendant on a gold chain from around her neck and put it on mine. My heart hurt upon saying goodbye and, as much as I wanted to leave, going off with this stranger felt to me as if I had been sold.

This was the last time I saw my brother-in-law. Shortly after I left, Macki was caught in a raid and deported. He was injured while escaping the deportation train during a bombardment of the allied forces, yet managed to come home to his young wife. They had neither food nor medication, and my sister went through a terrible time watching her husband succumb to his injuries. She was widowed at the age of nineteen.

I wanted my cousin Kurt, my best friend, to come along with me when I left Brussels, but his parents would not let him go. I was then sixteen years old; he was fifteen. We had always gotten along very well, and I was sure that together we could beat the odds.

My cousin Kurti who was like a brother to me.
He did not survive the Holocaust

Kurt, his sister Berta, and their parents all died together in a concentration camp. They were taken as a family directly from the train to the crematorium. I was told that, as they were getting off the train, my uncle refused to be separated from his children. He was a smart man, and probably thought he could protect them.

But they never had a chance. With one stroke of Hitler's inhumanity and his perpetrators, I lost my best friend, and with him, my childhood. Even today, when I close my eyes I can still see them. In winter, when fireplaces are lit, I don't see just the dancing flames—I see human skulls and mountains of ashes. To this day, historians squabble over the number of Jews who perished during the Holocaust. Does the number matter? Will more or less make the event less monstrous? Was my family counted?

When we were children, Kurt, my cousin and my friend, taught me to play soccer, and his all-boy team grudgingly accepted me. We spent so much time together that our parents, extended family, and friends teased us. But this did not diminish our friendship. He was the brother I wanted—we were happy and at peace in each other's company. We never quarreled; we seemed to be two souls each in search of the other. Vienna and its many parks were our playground. We went to different schools, but we often met in a park that was conveniently located between our two homes. We discussed and decoded the differences between our school experiences. In my public school, I met students of various religious denominations, young people who freely expressed their parents' prejudices against Jews. Kurt's parents believed that sending him to a Jewish academy would protect him from such experiences. I had my school friends and he had his, but the bond between us was never broken. We shared our secrets, wishes, and hopes, our sorrows and happiness. We even developed a secret form of writing, our own language that would prevent our parents and sisters from hearing us. As we grew older and became familiar with more parts of our city, we started to roam in wider circles. In the process, we discovered and befriended our cousin Ulli, who was our age and became the third member of our clan. The three of us were the youngest members of our large family. We were inseparable, The Three Musketeers. Ulli's parents managed to send him to England on one of the *Kindertransports*, and he survived; his parents disappeared in a concentration camp.

France

Stepping out once more with only a rucksack on my back, I left all my other possessions behind. I did not miss them. But I did miss my mother and the rest of my family, and all their love. My guide took me across the Belgian border into France, and then from one small village to the next, trying all the while to get rid of me somewhere. It soon became clear that she had no idea what to do. My brother-in-law had given her only half the fee she demanded; the rest of the money was in my possession with instructions to pay the guide when I had reached a safe place. Every day, she asked for the rest of the money but I was certain that once she was paid she would desert me; as difficult as it was I refused to pay.

The countryside was bristling with deserters and demilitarized French soldiers trying to get home. French police and German Gestapo were hunting for Jews to fulfill the daily deportation quotas demanded by the German Military Administration. My guide soon realized the danger she was in. We found out that raids were going on at all the major train stations: papers were checked, Jews and some French soldiers were arrested. The demilitarized French soldiers had already figured out what to do, and we followed their example. Trains were required to reduce their speed before entering a station: that was the time to jump on or off. We decided to get aboard the train to Paris, hoping the big city would be a safer place. Many people, including my guide and myself, jumped onto the train as it started to move out of the station.

The conductor never came through to check for tickets. He and the train's engineer showed compassion by slowing the train to a snail's pace a mile outside Paris. We all had plenty of time to get off. When we arrived in Paris, we were faced with a serious disappointment; the German military occupation was just as visible and dangerous as it had been in Brussels. We could not go to a regular hotel, where it would be necessary to relinquish all identification. The only places available to us were the small hotels where one paid by the hour: the brothels. Paris had many of them, and they were quite safe. After we arrived at a reasonable price for a night in one of these establishments, we could at least relax for a while. The next morning, my guide informed me that she could not go any further; she left without asking for the rest of the money. A brothel was not exactly the place I wanted to be, but no one bothered me and I needed time to rest and think. I arranged with the madam to stay for a few days.

I still had some of the food stamps my brother-in-law had bought on the black market, and I was very careful how I used them. One time, I treated myself to dinner in a restaurant. I ordered simply by pointing to the choice needing the fewest stamps. The plate arrived with a big cooked crab sitting atop it, with its claws extended. I had never eaten nor even seen a crab, and I had no idea what to do with it. Cautiously, I looked around to see what the other diners were doing; I saw that I would have to crack the crab's shell. *This I can do*, I thought. Daintily, I picked up the crab and bent back the claws, only to have the crab scrabble out of my hands and jump clear across to the next table. I had no idea it was necessary to hold tightly to the creature and actually kill it. I was very embarrassed, but tried to look as innocent as possible as I waited for the next course to be served.

Walking the city, keeping a careful lookout so as not to run into a raid, I searched for and found a coffeehouse where Jewish refugees congregated. As it was through most of my trek, I was the only girl in the crowd. I received much advice on how to proceed, some of it good, some of it not so good. I had to be very careful, and I knew I could not trust all I was told. Many people were more than willing to take advantage of a teenage girl. I had to depend on my own wits. Most of the men were very discouraged. Gestapo, French police, and anyone seeking to find favor with the Germans occupiers, any and all of these chased Jews. Our coffeehouse meetings had to be short: groups were too visible, and danger lurked all around. It was necessary to scrutinize every passerby; no one could be trusted. A few times I had the misfortune to get caught up in a raid, but I looked very young and, acting on impulse I was able to escape by casually attaching myself to some pedestrians, pretending to belong with them. Hopping just behind them, I received some astonished looks but was never rejected.

With the Gestapo breathing down my neck, my goal was to reach Free France and, from there, escape either to Spain or Switzerland. The hope of reaching Spain was very appealing, but my plan was quickly shattered. I had only summer clothes and wooden clogs, not exactly the outfit I would need to cross the Pyrenees.

Staying in Paris did not get me anywhere; after four days I left the city on foot, heading south. My ultimate goal was Switzerland. There were many displaced people on foot like me, and I soon got the hang of living on the road. The first day was the most difficult. I worried about where and how to find a safe place to sleep, until I remembered my mother telling me that a person in need could knock on any church door and ask to be taken in. I had nothing to lose. Before sunset I knocked on the door of one of the many churches I passed. To my surprise, I did not even have to ask for asylum; the person who answered the door immediately told me that I could stay for one night. He led me to the basement, where I found many other people in the same predicament. As far as I could judge, none were Jewish and all were men, most of them demilitarized French soldiers trying to find their way home. We each received a piece of bread and were told to leave early in the morning before the German military came to check the grounds.

Having been on the road for several weeks with false papers, a false name, a false place of birth, and pretending to be someone I was not, I needed to talk. I needed to tell the truth; for my mental health I needed to reclaim my identity. All the overnight guests were sleeping, except for a very young man sitting in a corner across from me. His eyes were wide open and feverish; it was obvious he could not sleep. We started whispering, both of us talking at the same time, words rushing from our lips, smiling with relief to be able to tell the truth without fear. I told him I was Jewish; he told me he had deserted his outfit. After a while I fell into an exhausted sleep. When I awoke, he was gone and, fearing for my life, I also left. Telling the truth was not advisable; it could get a person killed.

I continued south, through lovely French orchards and farmland. I had run out of food stamps and my diet consisted mostly of fruit, with the expected result. I needed solid food to settle my stomach. When it looked safe, I entered a bakery, stood in a corner until all shoppers disappeared, and only then begged for bread without stamps. This was dangerous for both of us, though the consequences would be different: the baker could go to jail, and I could lose my life.

Though I was mostly successful, I was always filled with fear at the need to approach strangers. Some local people and farmers were friendly and helpful. The difficulty was to find people who were opposed to the German occupation. But luck was with me. One time I stayed for several days at a farm, no questions asked. The middle-aged couple gave me shelter and food and treated me with kindness. There I was given my first good meal in a long time, although I became violently ill when I found out I had eaten the rabbit I had played with only a few hours before. When Sunday came I was asked to go to church with them; they had told their neighbors I was a relative from the city. With informers everywhere, it was safest to show up in church, as would be expected. I did as told, imitating all their actions. I met neighbors and friends, but I felt very uneasy, afraid of making a mistake.

I knew I could not continue this way. Next day I told the nice farmer and his wife that I had to leave. They wanted me to stay with them. When they realized I was serious, the farmer scouted out the neighborhood to find the safest way to the next village. By this time, security checks were set up on most country roads. The farmer gave it a lot of thought, finally deciding that the safest way would be simply to drive me through the checkpoints with a full wagon of hay. I sat next to the farmer on the driver's seat, in a disguise devised by his wife: an old kerchief, one of her old, worn sweaters, and hay sticking out all over my disheveled clothes. I thanked the farmer's wife, and we said good-bye.

After what seemed to be an eternity, we came to a checkpoint, where armed soldiers blocked the way and asked for identification. My throat closed up and my heart pounded in fear, as I presented my homemade identification papers. I smiled and chattered while the papers were scrutinized, and when they were handed back, we continued to the train station. I could not believe it: a complete stranger had risked his freedom, and possibly his life, to help me. To this day I wonder if the armed soldier did not see the primitive forgery of my papers, or did he simply not want to see?

The summer was passing. The days were getting shorter. I wondered what I would do once the winter set in. I had to hurry to arrive at a place where it was reasonably safe, where I would find other Jewish people, where I could get some idea of how to proceed. My progress was slow. I was not getting anywhere. It was time to take a risk. The express trains were too dangerous, full of military police checking for Jews and people without valid identification. The local trains connecting the farm towns were chugging along at a slow pace, at some spots coming nearly to a standstill. At these points, the refugees and the homeless waited to hop on. And so did I.

By now, I was used to traveling in cattle cars. There were always hands stretched out to help me up. Not knowing how long I would be on the road, I was very careful with my remaining money. I knew I would eventually need it to pay a smuggler to lead me into Switzerland. At several checkpoints armed German police boarded the trains; all of us without proper identification papers had to jump off. I was always scared to do this—What if I fell under the train?—but there was not much choice.

In this manner, I somehow arrived in Lyon in Free France, the southern part of the country under the Vichy government. To my great disappointment I learned that there was no freedom in "Free France." The Vichy government had an agreement with the Germans: They could govern what was considered the unoccupied part of the country as long as they cooperated with German demands. Secret police, informers and continuous raids harassed all of us.

My greatest desire was to be able to wash and sleep in a bed. In Lyon, I found an inexpensive room and paid for a few days. My financial situation was desperate. I had to find a way out before my funds were exhausted. The next task was to find where all the Jewish refugees congregated. This was easy—it was always a coffeehouse. It was dangerous to go there; big groups attracted the police, but I needed to stay informed. To my joy and surprise, I met my cousin Benno in a coffeehouse in Lyon. Independently of each other we had crisscrossed a very large portion of France. To meet this way seemed like a miracle, and it bolstered my courage. Benno, the family's daredevil, had recently checked out the situation at the Swiss border. It was heavily guarded, and anyone caught entering the country without a valid visa was transported without ceremony back to France. His advice to me was very valuable. It was not sufficient just to cross the border—it was necessary to walk as far into the interior as possible. Benno was going back to Paris, where he had left his wife hiding in a temporarily safe place. When he got there, they would try their escape together.

I let it be known that I was looking for a smuggler, someone familiar with the border area, to take me into Switzerland. Each day I visited the coffeehouse, which was still full of refugees, until I met a local man who seemed to be trustworthy. He wanted more money than I had, but he said he knew some other people who were interested and we could go as a group. I was not happy with this arrangement, because I believed that I had survived so far because I was alone. Groups and danger went hand in hand, but I had little choice, and I agreed.

Winter was just around the corner. I had no proper clothes, and I was at the end of my funds, with no family and no connections. This probably was my last chance to succeed. The smuggler picked the date, the night before Yom Kippur. I had misgivings, but the date was set.

Should I fast? Should I eat? In my already weakened condition, I could not go on such a stressful, risky, and arduous journey without eating. I had just enough money left to buy a loaf of bread and some cheese for a lonely meal in my room before departure. I reasoned that, since I was crossing the border illegally, I needed my strength, and that this could very well be my last meal. I thought of my family and wondered if I would ever see them again.

The smuggler and the group he assembled met at midnight. We were not permitted any luggage, and instructed not to make any noise. All of us were scared and very nervous. The family I was teamed up with never stopped talking, although they were reminded several times not to. I felt very vulnerable, and kept myself at a slight distance. We were told to walk in single line through the woods, but the group did not follow any instructions. It was pitch dark; it was spooky. We had to pass between enemy-occupied bunkers and find our way around guards with snarling dogs. We had to be careful not to step on any twigs, whose noise could give our presence away. It reminded me of my childhood, playing Indians in the woods near my home. But this was no game.

Our guide, unhappy with our noisy group, did not want to continue with us but pointed into the direction of Switzerland. I did not think this would end well, and I distanced myself even farther from the rest of the group. It was lucky that I did. Suddenly a loud voice shouted, "Halt!" The dogs were barking wildly. The group ran in all directions, with the dogs after them. I dropped to the ground and buried my face in the dirt. My mother's words rang in my ears: "Don't run from a dog," she used to tell me when I was a small child. "If you do, the dog will chase you." There was shooting and more ferocious barking, I didn't know what had happened, and I was too scared to look. I spent most of that night lying quietly on the ground, with my face in the dirt, hardly daring to breathe, and listening for the smallest sounds. Toward dawn, I got up to continue in the direction pointed out by the guide. I walked and walked until I left the woods behind. I had no idea where I was. Finally, I reached a picturesque community where the people seemed unconcerned with danger. All looked peaceful and normal. I did not see any guns, and I was nearly certain it was safe. Dirty and disheveled, I walked up to a policeman directing traffic, and told him my story.

Switzerland

Small and skinny, holding up my skirt so it wouldn't slip down my hips; I did not look like a girl of sixteen but more like a twelve-year-old child. I felt so very insignificant and, for the first time, really helpless. I had reached my goal; the only place in Europe not torn by war and hate. There was nothing I could do now to influence this man's decision over my life. Though I had not had any contact with my father, who resided in Zurich as a legal immigrant, I gave the officer my father's address. He held my hand while we walked to his station, where he made some phone calls. It was then decided that I should join my father in Zurich, and I was put on the train with a voucher to pay for my ticket. It was a strange experience. The language was unfamiliar, and the train took me to the German part of Switzerland. This was the part of the country that bordered on Austria, the country I had escaped from nearly four years earlier. As seen on the map, I had made a full circle, starting in Austria, then traveling through Germany, then Holland, Belgium, France, and Free France, then into Switzerland, which was uncomfortably near to Austria again. I was also anxious about meeting my father, whom I had not seen in several years. I saw him last when I was a child of twelve, and arrived in Zurich two months shy of my sixteenth birthday, experienced with warfare but little else.

My father Benjamin Jakob Rost as an older man

My father lived in a small-furnished room, and I was not permitted to stay with him. Nor did I wish to. The long separation had made us strangers. Jewish services were swamped with requests to find solutions for the many problems posed by a huge number of illegal Jewish refugees. They tried to find accommodations for all of us who were without money or possessions. I was boarded with a Jewish couple— who were originally from Russia—and their three adult, Swiss-born sons. They were good, generous, and kind people, initially somewhat disappointed when they saw me for the first time. They expected a nice teenager, not a ragamuffin experienced in survival and warfare. They spoke Russian-Yiddish and the local Swiss dialect, none of which I could understand. I felt very forlorn and lonely, and found it difficult to settle into a normal life. I was tense and very quiet, and had no idea about cooking or keeping house. My father came to visit on a weekly basis, but he was as much a stranger to me as the Swiss family; the long separation had destroyed our relationship. Slowly I came to realize that this could be where I would have to stay till the end of the war. I was restless, and when, after a few months, the Swiss authorities decided I should join the other illegal refugees in an internment camp, I was happy to comply, hoping to find people able to understand and relate with my experience and my fear of the future.

I packed my few accumulated possessions and set off to report to the camp. It was a large farm converted for wartime uses. Women and men were separated at night; we slept in different cowsheds, rows and rows of stables filled with straw. Fortunately, an elderly woman with two daughters took me under her wing on my arrival and showed me the ropes. We rose very early, then rushed outside and, with soldiers looking on, tried to wash at the trough normally used to water the animals. It was cold outdoors, the water was freezing, and it was nearly impossible to get clean. After a few days I learned to ignore the soldiers. We must have been their entertainment of the day. Each morning we used pitchforks to turn the straw serving as our mattresses. At the second gong we had to be ready for breakfast or we would miss the day's ration of bread. At the entrance to a large hall were two soldiers with baskets of bread. As we entered we each were given a quarter of a small round loaf to last us for the day. Some people ate their entire ration for breakfast. Though I was permanently hungry I decided to share my bread with a man I had met whom I trusted. I could manage on less, and he became my family and friend while we were locked up. All of us had to leave the buildings each afternoon for fresh air. Without my friend it was not safe for me, and the two of us always walked together. He was my protector. It was getting cold. I only had my few summer clothes and seeing all the internees smoking while outdoors I had the idea that the little fire could give me some warmth. It was a disappointing experience, and I decided to use the little money I had on extra food. There was nothing to do; time passed very slowly, and I was bored. One of the internees was a young doctor. She had the idea to start a school for some of us to fill the time. She taught anatomy and health, topics I have been fascinated with ever since. It was wonderful to be a student again, and I decided then that I would never stop learning.

As he had when I was staying with the Russian family, my father came to visit me every week. He always brought some food and, at my request, some books. It was such an odd experience to have my father standing on one side of a fence while I was on the other side being watched by an armed soldier. I was a prisoner in every sense. Did I truly break the law by trying to save my life? We all made the best of it, anyway. At least for the time being we were safe, although we feared that the war would eventually engulf all of us. The internment camp was near the border; we wondered what would happen should the Germans attack. One nightmare rumor was that all the Jews would be handed over in one neat package, as appeasement. I suppose it was not fair of us to think this; more and more people were trying to enter the country, and the Swiss were doing the best they could possibly do.

I, after my successful escape from Occupied Europe. (Photo taken in Switzerland, sometime in the middle of WWII)

The war continued, and Switzerland was an island of peace in a sea of chaos. When the camp became too crowded, the younger girls were removed to a place of their own; I had to move once more. Life was no easier in the new camp, but I have good memories from that place. We were housed in what was once a private school for girls, situated near Lausanne and overlooking the beautiful Lake Geneva. We had regular beds and——pleasure of pleasures—indoor bathrooms. We were organized into work teams, and took turns with cooking, washing, cleaning, waxing and polishing the wooden floors, and whatever else needed to be done.

One of the most difficult jobs was to break up the surface of the tennis courts so that vegetables could be planted. I absolutely could not manage the heavy pickax; it was taller and heavier than me. I was shown how to lift it high over my head, then let it come down under its own weight and power to do the job. It did not turn out this way, though. I lifted the pickax as high as possible, but I was unable to reverse the swing midway, and it came down behind my back with me lying on the floor. I was unhurt, and we all laughed. I was transferred to a different job that was equally tough but that didn't need as much muscle power. None of us resented the hard work. In exchange we had, for the first time, plenty of good food. Our supervisors were decent, and on weekends they took us on hikes into the woods to collect pine nuts and swim in the lake. The squirrels resented our intrusion, but we were promised that once we had a sufficient amount of nuts we could get Bircher-Muesli (a delicious Swiss cereal) for breakfast. It was a lovely setting, and for a while we were children again.

Too soon, though we were informed that the facility was needed for some other purpose, and we were split up and transferred to other camps. It was a sad goodbye; we had started to make friends. A very small group of us ended up in a secluded mountain lodge far away from even a small village. The first morning, I woke to the sound of cowbells and, looking out, saw a herd of cows in a bright green pasture. The sky was beautiful, and we were surrounded by mountains. I felt safe, but I wondered what I supposed to do. As in the previous camp, we were responsible for all the housework. After lunch we had free time, which had to be spent outdoors, and after dinner we had to knit socks. When knitting we had to sit ramrod straight, or we would get hit over the knuckles. I don't know how many pairs of socks I knitted; I have never knitted again. We spent most of our free time in the woods, again competing with the foraging squirrels. It was no hardship; we realized how lucky we were. We were hungry teenagers and the squirrels had no chance. When we had sufficient pine nuts we were again permitted to make muesli for breakfast. For sniffles or a sore throat we received the local treatment, a large raw onion. Except for worrying about my family and the future, it was a peaceful time.

While I was spending time in the various camps my father was working with the authorities to arrange my release. It was granted, and I was pleased to be freed; being moved from camp to camp was lonely and depressing. According to Swiss laws, I was too young to be permitted to live on my own. I had to go back to Zurich, and the family that had taken me in before graciously offered me asylum again. I had no money at all, but soon learned that I could work for the Jewish Family Services.

Together with many other workers, we all did the best we could. Many refugees needed to have their tattered clothes repaired. Most of the clothes were in shreds, which we patched as best we could. I considered it a labor of love. The pay was minimal, not enough to cover the cost of living, but it was enough for me to be able to rent a room of my own. It was small and unheated room, with basic furnishings including a basin, and a pitcher in which the water froze during the winter months.

The Swiss family was very good to me; they even took me along when they went on vacation. I was always welcome in their home. I did household chores and cooking in exchange for food and pocket money, and I was considered family. But was happy to be able to leave for my own place each night. None of the three young men in the family had a girlfriend, and it had become awkward. Their loving mother expected and asked me many times to choose one of her sons, but this was not what I wanted. She was a lovely old lady, and I felt ungrateful denying her wish. It was a difficult and stressful time. My life was on hold while the war was raging, yet I needed to become my own person before making any major decisions. The war continued, time passed. I would have liked to go back to school, but without money, it was impossible.

With all able-bodied men in the military, teenagers were asked to take up the slack at harvest time. I was assigned to a farm to pick grapes and apples and help the farmer's wife with chores. It was heavy, backbreaking work. We started early in the morning, with preparing a breakfast for the owners and their large crew. Huge amounts of potatoes had to have been prepared the evening before so they could be roasted in the morning. After scrubbing the huge, soot-covered pots and pans, I was told to pick grapes with the men until I was called in to help with preparing for lunch. Then I went out again to pick grapes until the wooden barrel on my back, with its leather straps cutting into my shoulders, was full. At that point, the barrel was emptied into a holding tank. After sunset I had to help cook dinner, wash the dishes, clean the huge pots again, and prepare the potatoes for the next day's breakfast.

On other days, I worked in the orchard collecting apples brought down by the wind—worms, dirt, and all—to be used in the making of cider.

I could not figure out if these farmers did not like Jews, or if they just did not like foreigners in general. All the hired men were given time to rest, yet I was working without ever getting a break. No one talked with me, and after many days of this treatment I decided to de-camp. Trying not to fall asleep after a day of heavy work, I waited for dark and, when all was quiet, took my suitcase and left. The door was creaking, but not even the dogs showed any sign of life. I reached the railroad station just in time to catch the last train out. The following day I went to the office where the farm assignments were made to register my complaint. I did not have to go back.

Life was routine until the doorbell rang one day. When I looked through the peephole, there was my cousin Benno grinning at me. He had been able to reunite with his wife, and they managed to get across the border into Switzerland. I was so happy; I could not believe he had found me. He and his wife were at a nearby internment camp. He had snuck out for an afternoon after learning that I was in Zurich.

A short time later, one other cousin was able to get into Switzerland, and he contacted me, as well. It felt so good not to be totally on my own, but to be part of a small family again. This cousin obtained permission to live with German refugees, a family with two young daughters who had a large apartment. One of them, Marga, was a red-haired beauty, and she and my cousin soon became engaged. They were married for many years.

Eventually the war ended, and we all had to think of our future. First, I wanted to find my family. As soon as traveling was permitted, I tried to get back to Belgium, but I was denied passage through France. The only way open to me was to fly from Zurich directly to Brussels. I had saved, with great difficulty, some of the money I earned all these years. I had just enough to pay for my ticket. I had never flown; the plane was a leftover relic of the war, with no seats and no regulated air pressure. It was a most uncomfortable, bumpy, scary flight. After we landed, I tumbled out, green in the face and nearly unable to walk.

I could hardly wait to see my mother, my sister and the rest of my family. My mother was one of nine siblings, all of them married. I had eight uncles, eight aunts, and nineteen cousins. Most of them had perished during the war, my wonderful friends whom I had grown up with. My immediate family—my parents, my sister, and I—were the only ones to have survived intact. I mourned my brother-in-law and all the rest of my family and friends for a long, long time.

Slowly some survivors came back, many of them broken in body and in spirit. One of these was a young man named Karl. He and my sister dated for a few months, then decided to marry and emigrate to Argentina, which was, at the time, the only country willing to accept Jews.

We had survived. We had "won." But at what cost? Soon it was time to leave. My two-week visitor's visa gave us hardly enough time to get to know each other again.

But this time, leaving was easier. My mother promised to come and visit, and Grete came on her own twice to see me in Switzerland. It was wonderful to be together and have a sister again. We tried to recapture our youth. I was very sad when Grete and Karl came once more to say goodbye before leaving for Argentina. There was no certainty that we would ever see each other again.

During my short visit in Belgium, I had also met a little cousin, Aunt Jenny's child. I was told that when the German soldiers came to take my aunt she cried and screamed as loud as she could, so they would not hear the crying baby under the bed. Some neighbors saved the little girl and handed her over to the Jewish community. The Jewish organizations tried to find a family for her. I think at the time I met her she was maybe six years old; she was a sad little girl. We all felt terrible not being able to keep her. None of us had a home. All of us were on the way to somewhere else, and none of us had any money. We were completely dependent on the goodwill of strangers. As far as I know, my little cousin was taken to England when I returned to Switzerland. At the time I thought we would meet again, but it did not turn out this way. We all ended up in different parts of the world. Life was very difficult, and we lost her. I don't know how she ended up in England; I hope she found a good family to take her in. It is terrible to grow up lonely and without love. We never heard from her mother, my Aunt Jenny, again.

Now that the war had ended, I applied and was granted a work permit. I was twenty-one years old and had come of age. I started going out with friends, exploring the city of Zurich and some of the beautiful

Swiss countryside with my cousins. On Sundays, some of the great hotels of the city had afternoon tea with music and dancing. I loved to dance and enjoyed the elegant atmosphere, a much-needed break from my dreary one-bedroom quarters.

As she had promised, my mother arrived after some time. She and my father tried to pick up their relationship, but the eight-year separation could not be bridged; they had grown apart. Though my mother only had a visitor's visa, the Swiss authorities relented and let her stay in the country. I was very happy to have her with me, but there was no space for her in my tiny room. We did not have the money or the necessary permit to get an apartment, so we lived in separate places. It was a difficult time. We had all been through so much during the years we had been separated. We had to get to know each other again, and find our common denominator. I had truly changed, I was a grown young woman and could not relate to my mother the way I did when I was fifteen. She was sad, hopeless, and marked by the hardships she had endured. We talked about the war, our lost family members and what the future could hold for us. She was not at all happy about my stagnant life. I was not exactly thrilled either but saw no options to change it.

Once I took my mother to an afternoon tea. As the music started, a young man named Janos approached me asked me to dance. In the Yiddish language there is a word, *beschert*, that means "It is meant to be." That same young man and I have been married now for more than sixty years. Of course, we did not know at the time what the future held for us, but when Janos asked me to go out on a date, I accepted. He was a college student, had one more year of school. He wanted to emigrate once he finished his studies. He had relatives in the United States, England, Uruguay, and Israel. I had relatives in The United States, England, Argentina, and Israel.

I did not even think of going anywhere; I did not want my mother to be left all alone. She had different ideas, though. As soon as she had arrived in Switzerland, she had applied for a visa to the United States in my name; if the time ever came, she thought if ever, I could make up my mind to go or stay. Only when my signature was needed did she inform me of her actions. It was a courageous and clever move, and I will be forever grateful to her. Just as she had sent me on my way from Belgium many years before, she again was willing to let me go to find a better life. The visa arrived after my cousin, Rosa, in Washington agreed to be responsible for my financial upkeep in the United States. It was a necessary step; no entry was permitted without it. When I applied for a stateless travel document, called a *Nansen* passport, I was told, to my surprise that because I had lived in Switzerland for nearly ten years, I was eligible to apply for Swiss citizenship. The Austrian government also invited me to return to Austria. Though I was pleased to be asked, the thought of returning to the country responsible for so many deaths, and the destruction and exile of my family and me, was abhorrent. By then I was twenty-five years old. I was poor, and had no prospects and no professional skills; I could not afford an apartment, and I did not want to live like this forever. Most of the people I knew, including Janos, had already left; I was tired of Europe, tired of being an outsider, to be forever considered a bloody foreigner, as they say in Switzerland a *Chaibe Uslander.* The summer of 1950, I set out for Washington, D.C.

America

It was difficult to once more say goodbye to my mother. My future was not clear. I had no idea what to expect from life in America, and we were wondering if we would ever see each other again. The train took me from Zurich through France, with a short stop in Paris to meet some fellow travelers. Every one of us was emigrating to America. In Le Havre, we boarded the ship to take us across the ocean.

It was a stormy crossing; the tables and chairs in the dining room had to be bolted down. Ropes were strung across open areas for us to hold on to. I shared my cabin with a woman I had never met before. Both of us were wildly, continuously seasick. It finally dawned on me that the fresh air up on deck was the best cure for seasickness, and I spent several days gripping the rails without looking at any person showing intention to be sick. The storm ended as suddenly as it had started, but the small ship continued rocking on huge waves. I thought I would take a shower, as most of the people were huddled, miserable and sick, in their bunks. With no one lining up to use the showers, this was my opportunity, or so I thought. It was not such a good idea.

When I was ready to leave the shower I found, to my distress, that the storm had damaged the door and it was jammed shut: there was no way I could get out. I had a large towel, but my clothes were out of reach. It took some time before my roommate missed me, but she brought a repairman to take the door off its hinges. While I was waiting, I had plenty of time to think of all possible terrible situations. What if the storm started again? What if the boat sank and no one came looking for me? But all's well that ends well; it was *beschert,* ordained that I should live.

Land-ho! The Statue of Liberty, New York, hope, fear, uncertainty, immigration officers, debarking, finding my luggage. The ship had docked in a downpour, in the midst of a strike. There were no porters to unload luggage, no taxis, and no welcome for the weary travelers. The New World did not salute me upon my arrival. I did not speak English; I just had an address to go to, and no idea how to get there. I was quite forlorn. Finally, I asked one of the stewards for help. He found me a cab and I showed the drive my paper with the address.

My father's older sister and her family had left Europe before World War II started. They had lived in New York for years, and were American citizens. I did not have their home address, but I did have the address of their store, so that was where I went. They were very religious, and there was no joy in seeing me, no questions about my parents or their own younger sister. My father, a non-religious free thinker, had been cast out by his family and, with him, all of us. They were relieved to hear that I wanted to continue to Silver Springs,

Maryland, and only needed help to get there. I was given a ticket and put on the train. In Silver Springs, I was received with open arms by my mother's only surviving sister and her two married children. Her son and his wife, Marga, had left Switzerland sometime before I did. Her daughter Rosa, had somehow managed to arrive in America, by way of England, in the middle of the war and was married to an American. I lived with them until I found work and earned enough money to rent a place of my own.

My first job was to learn English. Marga's mother (I called her *Oma*—grandmother—Lina) and I took a night course titled "English for Foreigners." *Oma* Lina used to joke about the fact that despite the wide difference in our ages, we were going to school together. At this course we met students of all ages and from all over the world. Our teacher not only instructed us in the ways of American life but also gave us back our self-confidence and courage.

After I found my way around town, I needed to tackle life. Cousin Marga came with me to fill out a job application form at the Woodward and Lothrop Department store in Washington, D.C., where I was hired as a sales clerk. I could not have done this without her help and the support of my other relatives. Far from perfect in speaking or understanding English, I often had no idea what my customers wanted to purchase but with a lot of pointing, smiling and bringing just about everything out I somehow managed and learned. It made my job difficult, exciting and at times truly funny.

As soon as I had employment, I applied for my first papers to become an American citizen. These papers enabled me later to sponsor my mother, my sister, and my brother-in-law Karl to come to the United States.

Aunt Hilda, one of my mother's sisters, and my cousins were very loving and helpful, but I was lonely. I had been on my own for so many years; I felt I did not fit in anywhere. Sponsored by his sister, Benno and his wife had also arrived in the U.S. and lived in New York City. I was drawn to Benno; we could talk about our past, our lost family. He had known me as a small child, and though he was much older, I loved him and knew him well. I could hardly wait for Friday evenings. Many times I got on the train to New York immediately after work, to spend the weekend with Benno and his wife. It was the first time I felt at home since I was a child.

Janos had left Switzerland a few months before I did, and lived in Canada. He was just as lonely as I. We wrote back and forth continually, until finally we decided to get married. I arranged all the necessary paperwork, and Aunt Hilda knew an Orthodox rabbi from Vienna. Janos arranged for a two-week visitor's visa to the U.S. His passport had a notation: "Entry permitted for the purpose of marriage only." We had a good laugh about that.

So, early one morning we went to court, to be married by a judge. then, in the afternoon, we saw the rabbi in his office. He was annoyed that we had seen the judge before him, but he nevertheless, after many questions, performed the ceremony and pronounced us man and wife.

My cousins gave a party, inviting all their friends—to this day, I have no idea who was there. All of them were kind strangers bearing gifts. We spent our honeymoon in New York, visiting museums, parks, and the opera, where we saw a wonderful performance of *Porgy and Bess.* Two weeks passed very quickly, and we had to say goodbye again. Janos had to go back to Canada, and I started procedures to get a Canadian visa. It took a while before the paperwork was finalized, but that gave me time to adjust to a new move. Finally the day arrived, and I again said goodbye. An official inspected my stateless, *Nansen* passport at the Canadian border. He handed it back to me, and I nearly burst into tears. But there was a printed piece of paper inserted in the passport. It said, "There are no second-class citizens in our country." These were the first kind and positive words I had heard from a public figure since I left Vienna. What a wonderful welcome!

Canada

Getting off the train in Montreal in the middle of winter, I was happy and pleased to see my husband but shocked by the incredible cold. I was coming directly from Washington, D.C., and I had no idea that the climate could be so different. I was wearing nylons, a short jacket; I had neither hat nor boots, and I could feel my nylons freezing to my skin. I had never felt so cold before. The next day, we shopped for a fur-lined coat and found a good deal: I wore it for many, many years. We started our married life in a small town in Quebec, where Janos had found work. Our rented one-bedroom apartment was identical to a dozen others in the building. All had the same floor plan and the same furniture, including the same rocking chair. From six p.m. to midnight the whole building creaked, with all the rocking chairs going. It drove me absolutely crazy.

It was a truly small town. Except for the one factory that had hired Janos sight unseen, there was nothing there. There was no reason for us to stay. I had heard on the radio that McGill University in Montreal was making scholarships available, but I needed the help of a friend to convince Janos to apply. He was reluctant to give up the security of his employment, but eventually agreed that there was no future for him in this job in this tiny town. We were extremely lucky; he received a four-year renewable scholarship to study for his Ph.D. in chemistry. I clerked for an insurance company, checking applications, typing, figuring out rates, and collecting payments. When applying for this position I felt duty-bound to mention that I was a slow typist, but that in exchange I made no mistakes. The workplace was pleasant, and I enjoyed the friendship of my colleagues. My salary was average, but it barely paid for the necessities. I stayed at this job until Janos graduated from the university.

We lived in a mansard on Sherbrooke Street just across McGill and were hopeful about our future.

Montreal was full of young refugees from every country of Europe. All of us were poor, but all were resolved to succeed. Our friends were Polish, German, Austrian, Indian, Greek, Swiss, Jamaican, and Hungarian and, after a while, even some Canadians. We organized a breakfast club, and each Sunday many of us congregated at the chosen diner for breakfast, where we shocked the waitress by ordering a huge number of croissants and endless cups of coffee. Soon many small foreign restaurants and coffeehouses began to open, and it was very obvious that the refugees had made an impact on Montreal. The city was in transition. It was an interesting time.

Janos graduated *magna cum laude*, receiving his Ph.D. in only three years. According to his professor, Dr. Mason, it was an unheard-of achievement. After the graduation exercises, Prof. Mason, a kindly man, said that Janos had received his Ph.D., but that I had earned a Ph.D.:

"Putting Hubby Through." Now came the search for employment. Economically and politically 1954 was not a good time, but luck and his professors' connections prevailed, and shortly after graduation Janos (now John), started to work for the Pulp and Paper Company of Canada. Again we found ourselves in a small, rural, one-company town, this time in Hawkesbury, Ontario. The company practically owned the town, and it watched benevolently over its employees. We had the choice of a company-owned apartment or house, either for the sum of fifty dollars per month. Most of the lower management employees with children had chosen a house in a nice suburban setting and, even though we had no children at the time, we also opted for a house.

To move from one bedroom to a two-story house was a drastic change. We needed everything. Mostly we needed a car so John could get to work. The salary was appropriate for a new Ph.D. graduate: much more than I had brought home previously, but barely enough for all the new expenses. We lived frugally, from month to month. Main Street had one food store, a nice ladies' dress store, a hardware store, a men's store, a bakery and ice cream store, and a government-run liquor store. Outside the company there were no jobs available and I could not find employment within a reasonable distance.

We settled down to company life and found good friends, but we were the only Jews in town. As was customary, the local Catholic priest came to visit us after a few weeks to find out why he had not seen us in church. It turned out that being Jewish was an acceptable explanation, but some of our friends, being Greek Orthodox, were not so fortunate.

The priest visited them every week for a long time. He was a nice man and tried his best, but he finally gave up. The company also owned a golf course, and employees were permitted to play once a week without charge. We took advantage of this opportunity whenever possible—we even received free lessons—but we did not show much aptitude. We were invited to company-sponsored dinner parties, which we were expected to attend. Life was good, but we felt watched. I was told it was customary to leave the window curtains open. I did not comply: my curtains stayed closed. Eventually I realized that the attention we received was well meant, but at the time my experiences during the war still affected my judgment, and too much attention put my nerves on edge.

We missed our exciting life in Montreal and often went to visit our friends Pierrette and Steve for the weekend. They, in turn, came to see us. Most of our friends were refugees with no extended families; we truly needed each other. We talked much about the past, how we survived, what we expected from the future and how to attain our goals.

Grete and Karl could not adjust to life in Argentina; after the war, the government had accepted not just Jews but also many German Nazis and the future did not look good. Also, my sister's health was in jeopardy; one German doctor in Buenos Aires told her she needed surgery to remove a tumor. Fortunately, Karl and Grete received their visas just in time, and upon arriving in the United States found out that my sister was expecting a baby. There was no tumor! To the joy of his parents—and us!—my nephew David was born several months later.

Our joy was heightened when my mother's visa was also finally approved. After her arrival she lived with Karl and my sister in New York, and was overjoyed with her first grandchild.

Sadly, Karl was not able to forget his nightmarish experiences of the Holocaust and concentration camps, and found it difficult to adjust to life in America. Learning a new language, adjusting to new customs, it was all overwhelming to him. The stress of adjusting to a new life and providing for a family was too much. He succumbed to depression, and died without seeing his beloved son grow up.

I truly wanted to have children, to create a new life that would help us to put the Holocaust behind us. To my delight, I became pregnant; to my dismay, there was no hospital in our company town. There was a doctor in a nearby town, but the nearest hospital was one hour away in another small town. We decided to make the trip to Montreal for my check-ups. It was a long drive, but we had found a modern facility and it was worth the trip. The only problem was the time it took to get there, so I spent the ninth month of my pregnancy on my own, in a small rented room near the hospital.

John came to visit me on weekends. This was a very difficult time for me. But even though it was not the best of situations, it turned out to be the right choice. My daughter Jessica was born healthy, at nearly six pounds. I developed childbed fever, however. I was treated with penicillin, and had an allergic reaction. It was very important to be in a modern hospital.

At the time childbirth was not covered by insurance, and baby Jessica could not leave the hospital before all bills were paid. Only cash was accepted, no checks. We were desperate; we simply did not have enough cash. Our good friends, Pierrette and Steve, bailed us out. For many years, they joked that they had paid for her, and that therefore Jessica was partly theirs.

I was notified of my father's death shortly after my daughter was born; life and death within the same week. The war had made us strangers, but I was very sad.

Parenthood did not come easy. Jessica was very tiny and needed to be fed every two hours. After a few months I was so tired I asked the pediatrician if he could give the baby some medication to help her sleep through the night. He was compassionate and prescribed sleeping tablets, but not for the baby—for me. Without any family to help I appreciated the many visits from our friends. They came often and helped in every way. We became Canadian citizens and were proud of it. It felt so special to belong.

John enjoyed his work. The Pulp and Paper Institute of Canada had hired many of the young new graduates from all the corners of the world. All of them were intelligent and ambitious. Our social life was interesting, but we chafed under the small-town atmosphere. Additionally, there was no chance of advancement with so many smart young scientists in one company. One by one, most of our new friends found new and better jobs in other locations. We discussed following their example, and John applied for and was offered employment at the

Rohm and Haas Company in Philadelphia. We were overjoyed, although there was one complication. Having been born in Budapest, John fell under the Hungarian quota, which was filled. In 1958 Hungarians, could not enter the United States except by special dispensation. We were greatly relieved and happy when the Rohm and Haas Company arranged for us to get this dispensation by stating in an affidavit that John was the only scientist they had found for their research project.

I had loved living in Canada and was sad to be moving again.

Return to the US

Having lived in the United States before, I had no problems re-entering the country, even though I fell under the Austrian quota. So while John gave notice at Pulp and Paper, finished his research project, and waited for his visa to come through, I traveled to Philadelphia to find a place for the three of us. I rented a car for myself and Baby Jessica, and we had a little adventure on our way south. I had never driven an American car, and as it became dark, I discovered with a shock that the lights were not where I expected them to be. I pushed and pulled every visible button, but nothing happened. I drove through deserted, dark country roads until I reached a gas station and got help from the people there.

With John's new salary of $9,600 per year it was difficult to find a home we could afford. We did not have many options, and after a few days of comparisons I rented a house in Levittown, Pennsylvania, a bedroom community of simple homes, thirty minutes outside Philadelphia. With many of John's new colleagues living there, he could carpool to work, leaving the car for my use.

We socialized with John's colleagues and baby-sat for each other. Nearly all of Levittown's homeowners were young families, soldiers back from the war who had bought their house with a G.I. loan. We lived there for several years without ever meeting any other Europeans.

Initially, the American way of life was strange to us but we soon fitted in. The only thing I could never get used to was the rows and rows of identical houses. Ours was the eighth from the corner and at night I had to count houses to find my home. Later, I just looked for my next-door neighbor's red drapes, but my luck ran out the day she opted for new colors. After driving up and down the street I had to go back to the corner to one more count houses.

John's parents survived the Holocaust in Hungary. After the war they went to Israel, where they lived for a few years and even established a small business. They wanted us to come to Israel but I desperately craved peace and, having moved so often, had neither energy nor nerve for more upheaval. Daily news reports made it clear there would be war in Israel. Wanting to be with us, they sold their business and came to Montreal. They were disappointed when we moved to the United States; they followed us after some time, and settled in New York, where we visited them often. It was a long drive from Philadelphia; we usually saw my family in the morning, John's family in the afternoon, then we drove home. I never really got to know New York.

Jessica was three and a half years old when our son was born on July 28, 1959. Again, the hospital was in the next town, but it was not very far. Freddy, a large and happy baby, weighed a full nine pounds at birth. We were Canadian citizens, at the time, and with our harrowing European experience, I wanted the whole family to belong to the same country; I feared separation. With Jessica having been born in Canada, we decided to register Freddy as a Canadian citizen born to Canadian parents abroad.

We became infected with the American dream for a house and took advantage of the Rohm and Haas Company's saving plan. Each month, a large amount of John's salary was withheld, while we tried to manage as frugally as before. By 1961 we finally had the money for a down payment and the search began. It was an exciting time; we found the house of our dreams. Cheltenham was a small, old town with good schools just a few minutes from Philadelphia. We had the benefit of both small-town living and big city activities, a university, and wonderful museums. In 1963, all of us became American citizens. We lived for many years in Cheltenham.

Once both children were in school, I applied and passed the entrance exams to Temple University. I thought to myself, "Now certainly it will be my turn to fulfill a dream." Many evenings the children and I sat around the table doing our homework together. I was interested in medical technology.

But it was not meant to be. I had been at the university for only two years when John was offered a much better position with the American Can Company in New Jersey. We were all sad to leave Cheltenham and our many friends, but it did get us nearer to our families in New York. We found a house in Westfield, New Jersey, just a thirty-minute drive west of New York. Our children were very happy there, and we all enjoyed the easy access to the city. This was our fifth move since we had married, and three more were to follow. Having come to the conclusion that my children's future was of greater importance than my desire for achievement, I never went back to finish my studies. I went to work, instead. We saved my salary, and I am very proud that I was able to pay for our daughter's college education.

John became a successful research scientist and later vice president of a large company. I achieved what I had wished for when I started on the trek to save my life: a family, children, and grandchildren. They are my link to immortality.

Oh yes, this is our home, we are happy to be American citizens.

Why Write Now

The Second World War and the Holocaust happened a long time ago, yet there were always people who denied—and still deny—its occurrence. It was easy to refute such accusations when there were so many of us who knew differently, but after all these years there are very few survivors left. Antisemitism has begun to raise its ugly head again. I considered myself lucky to have survived, and I never talked much about my personal experience. But the dead cannot speak; I am ninety-two years old, and I feel compelled to tell my story. It is not a story of heroics, but of random luck and perseverance.

Epilogue I

To my mother I give thanks for the courage she instilled in me, letting me know that I could rise to any challenge. Of the forty-eight people I called my family, only twelve survived the Holocaust. I have never forgotten any of them, and it still hurts. This was not a war of one nation against the other. It was cold-blooded murder. Today's young people take the existence of Israel for granted and do not understand its importance. Europe's Jewish people were chased and hunted like animals. Those who lost their lives, as well as we, the survivors, had no one to speak for us. As long as there is Israel this will never happen again.

My Mother Manja Rost, my sister Grete, and I

When I remember my childhood, I see my cousins Kurt and Berta and their parents going into the gas chambers holding onto each other. Siggy also died during the war. My grandfather was hidden with a family in Antwerp. One day, I was told, he combed his long beard and *peyes* (side locks), put on his hat and defiantly walked out the door. He was never heard of again. I remember him as a tall, strong, open-minded man. When I close my eyes I can still see the faces of my many uncles, aunts, and cousins who perished in German concentration camps.

Many years after I was forced to leave, I visited the country of my birth. Austria is beautiful, yet I had very mixed feelings and counted the days to my departure. The following words describe the emotional impact this trip had on me

Where ever I move space opens—
Emptiness surrounds me—I am alone
With excitement rising
I am looking for my past.

Yet silence shouts from empty halls,
Echoes from wall to wall—
Nobody home—all are gone.
I ring the bell, but walls are of stone.

A whisper remains of words once dear,
Like a half-forgotten tune,
Sometimes gentle, sometimes loud,
Only for me to hear.

September 2011

Epilogue II

I began to write a long time ago, and little by little came to the end, or so I thought, when something totally unexpected happened. I was in the habit, while sitting at my computer of looking, without expectation, at a list of photos being shown by the Holocaust Museum titled *Remember Me?* Suddenly, one day, there was the picture of my little cousin as I had remembered her all these years. Her name, place of birth, origin, mother's first name—my Aunt Jenny—it all fit. After contacting the person in charge, Dr. Jude Richter, our combined information made it a fact: "Jeannette" was indeed my little lost cousin. More than sixty-five years have passed since the end of World War II. If she had married, what would be her name? And where in the world had she settled? Dr. Richter asked for permission to put my story on television and hope for the best.

Then we waited. And just when I had about given up, he called triumphantly. My cousin's daughter was amazed to see her mother's childhood picture on public TV. They live in England and now that we have made contact, a visit was planned.

It was early in the year of 2012 that my cousin Jeannette and her daughter Susan arrived. Though she looked very different from the baby picture that I remembered, I had no problem recognizing her. She looks so very much like her mother, my Aunt Jenny. We had a wonderful reunion. My daughter took a few days of vacation to meet Jeannette and Susan, and it was uncanny how much alike the young people are. I am happy to have found Jeannette and also sad thinking of all the time that has passed without knowing her. Her childhood was as I had feared, lonely, forever hoping to find her family. She vaguely remembers meeting an elderly lady named Lotte, my mother (not her legal name but one my mother preferred). Jenny gave me a photograph and asked, "Have you any idea who these people are?" I could hardly believe my eyes: The people in question were my sister and me. We hope to get together again, but for the time being email and letters will do.

I am extremely grateful to the Holocaust Museum in Washington for showing the list of child survivors, *Remember Me?* and to Dr. Jude Richter for the work he did to make this reunion possible.

January 2017

An Unexpected Experience

It was several years after the end of World War II before I finally received a visa to the United States. With only a few words of the language, I felt like a fish out of water. At the time, very few people wanted to hear of the Holocaust. New, well-meaning new American friends and acquaintances advised me regularly to forget the past. But how does one forget the past? How does one forget half of one's life? Is not our experience that makes us who and what we are? One day, I thought, I will write my story.

As my language skills improved I became able to read the books of many great writers, and I wondered what I could say that had not been said before and much better than I could ever tell it. Who needs another Holocaust story? But the past is never forgotten. My war experience was a heavy weight on my soul. It did not let me sleep; memories popped up at the oddest moments.

A few years ago I started to write. Never more than a few sentences; at the most half a page. And now I am finished. The last time I looked at my story was to proofread it, and this was when I had an unexpected experience. Reading my memoirs, I became aware that the past, though not forgotten, has no hold on me anymore. I am a different person, speak a different language, live a different life. Writing my story has cleansed my soul.